D1532491

The North American Indians

Native Americans
of the Great Lakes

Titles in The North American Indians series include:

The Cherokee
The Comanche
Native Americans of the Great Lakes
The Navajo
The Sioux

The North American Indians

Native Americans
of the Great Lakes

P.M. Boekhoff and Stuart A. Kallen

KIDHAVEN
PRESS™

THOMSON

GALE

San Diego • Detroit • New York • San Francisco • Cleveland
New Haven, Conn. • Waterville, Maine • London • Munich

© 2004 by KidHaven Press. KidHaven Press is an imprint of The Gale Group, Inc.,
a division of Thomson Learning, Inc.

KidHaven™ and Thomson Learning™ are trademarks used herein under license.

For more information, contact
KidHaven Press
27500 Drake Rd.
Farmington Hills, MI 48331-3535
Or you can visit our Internet site at http://www.gale.com

LIBRARY OF CONGRESS CATALOGING-IN-PUBLICATION DATA

Boekhoff, P.M. (Patti Marlene), 1957–
    Native Americans of the Great Lakes / by P.M. Boekhoff and Stuart A. Kallen.
    p. cm. — (The North American Indians)
  Summary: Discusses Native Americans of the Great Lakes region and their customs,
  family life, organizations, food gathering, beliefs, housing, and other
  aspects of daily life.
  Includes bibliographical references and index.
    ISBN 0-7377-1510-3 (alk. paper)
  1. Indians of North America—Great Lakes—History—Juvenile literature.
  2. Indians of North America—Great Lakes—Social life and customs—Juvenile
  literature. [1. Indians of North America—Great Lakes.] I. Kallen, Stuart A., 1955–
  II. Title. III. Series.
    E78.G7B64   2004
    977.004'97—dc22
                                                                        2003017763

Printed in the United States of America

Contents

Chapter One 6
People of the Lakes

Chapter Two 15
Family Life

Chapter Three 23
Beliefs and Ceremonies

Chapter Four 31
Conflict with Settlers

Glossary 41

For Further Exploration 42

Index 44

Picture Credits 47

About the Authors 48

Chapter One

People of the Lakes

The Great Lakes are made up of five large, connected lakes that lie near the northeastern end of the border between the United States and Canada. They contain the world's largest body of freshwater. Millions of people now live around the Great Lakes in more than a dozen large industrial cities.

Hundreds of years ago Native Americans lived all along the Great Lakes, surrounded by forests of oak, pine, birch, and elm. The forests teemed with wildlife, including squirrels, deer, bears, and elk. The lakes were filled with many kinds of fish and shellfish.

The people of the Great Lakes lived in dozens of different tribes, or large family groups. Although each tribe had its own culture and customs, most tribes spoke one of two languages. The tribes who lived around present-day Lakes Erie, Michigan, and Superior spoke one of the Algonquian (al-GAHN-kwi-an) languages. Those who lived farther east, around Lakes Ontario and Huron, spoke one of the Iroquois (IR-uh-kwoy) languages.

The People of the Longhouse

The Iroquois tribes, known as the Six Nations, were the most powerful in the eastern region of the Great Lakes.

Dozens of Native American tribes once lived along the forested shores (pictured) of the five Great Lakes (inset).

The six tribes were called Cayuga, Mohawk, Oneida, Onondaga, Seneca, and Tuscarora. They lived mostly in present-day New York state and around Lake Ontario in Canada. Another Iroquois-speaking nation called the Huron lived near Lake Huron. The Huron were not part of the Six Nations. In fact, the Six Nations became powerful enemies that were often at war with the Huron.

Because the tribes of the Six Nations lived in log homes called longhouses, they called themselves the "People of the Longhouse." Longhouse villages were often located where two streams ran together. These villages were connected by trails that wound through the woods. People in each village lived in longhouses made from elm poles covered with sheets of elm bark. Longhouses were about 25 feet wide and up to 150 feet in length. The roof of the longhouse was arched and about 25 feet high at its center.

Longhouse villages were often built where two streams ran together.

A longhouse is made of elm poles covered with sheets of bark.

As many as seven families—up to fifty people—lived in each longhouse. Each family had its own fire pit, spaced about twenty feet from the next. A hole in the roof above every pit acted as a chimney, letting out wood smoke while allowing light into the longhouse. Storage baskets, full of dried fruit and corn, squash, beans, and tobacco, swung from wooden hooks pounded into the roof beams.

The Iroquois thought of their hundreds of villages as one large family, or nation. They called their nation the Iroquois League. The Iroquois League reached all the way across New York. It was governed by a Grand **Council** of fifty chiefs called sachems. The chiefs were responsible

An Ottawa chief speaks with tribal members seated around a campfire.

for keeping peace, speaking for the tribes to outsiders, and helping the league act together in case of war. When major issues were decided, nothing could be done unless all the sachems agreed to a course of action.

The Three Fires

The Algonquian-speaking people, who lived to the west of the Iroquois, originally called themselves the Anishinabe. According to legend, they moved from the Atlantic region to the western Great Lakes long ago. When they moved from east to west, they kept their campfires burning from the embers of one original fire. Along the way, the Anishinabe split into three groups, known as the "Three Fires." These tribes were the Ottawa, the Potawatomi, and the Ojibwa (also known as Ojibway or Chippewa).

Each tribe had an important special role in the Three Fires group. The Ottawa specialized in trading with other tribes. The Potawatomi kept and guarded the sacred fire of peace. This means they brought the tribes together for feasts and meetings called councils where they discussed and solved problems. The Ojibwa, the largest and most powerful tribe around the Great Lakes, kept the sacred ideas and spiritual beliefs of the people alive in stories, songs, and pictures painted or carved into birch bark.

Wild Rice and Fish

As they moved to the western part of the Great Lakes, the Ojibwa received a spiritual prophecy, or prediction. This message from the gods stated that if the tribe kept moving west, the people would find a place where food grew on the water. The prophecy came true when the Ojibwa reached the thousands of small lakes found near Lake Superior and northern Lake Michigan. These lakes provided a rich source of wild rice, a cereal grain like wheat that grows in shallow water.

This area was also home to the Menominee. Menominee means "good berry," an Indian name for wild rice. Because the grain was plentiful, it was central to Menominee society. The surrounding land also contained copper that tribe members made into jewelry, bowls, and other items.

The Menominee were longtime friends and trading partners with another tribe in the region. The Winnebago lived in present-day Wisconsin on the western edge of Lake Michigan, where fish were plentiful. (Today, the Winnebago are known as Ho-Chunk. This is their ancient name taken from words meaning "first voice" or "great fish nation.")

Although they lived among the Algonquian speakers, the Winnebago spoke a language of the Lakota and Dakota tribes who lived west of the Great Lakes. Like the Lakota, the Winnebago hunted buffalo on the Great Plains. They often turned the buffalo skins into warm robes and traded them with the Menominee.

The Southern Shores

Many other tribes lived in Wisconsin and on the southern shores of the Great Lakes. One tribe, the Fox, called themselves the Mesquakie, or "Red Earth People." The Sac, or Sauk, were the "Yellow Earth People." In the sum-

An Ojibwa family returns to their lakeside settlement. The Ojibwa were the most powerful tribe around the Great Lakes.

Building an Iroquois Wigwam

3. Frame is covered with woven reed mats.

2. Frame is tied together with rope-like wood fibers.

1. Flexible tree branches are placed in the ground in an oval shape and pulled together in arches.

mer, the Fox farmed the red soil of eastern Wisconsin and the Sac farmed the yellow-colored land to the north along the western edge of Lake Michigan.

Although they came from many different tribes, the Native Americans along the southern shores of the Great Lakes lived in a similar manner. In the summer, they stayed in longhouses and other large wooden buildings. In winter, some tribes left their villages to settle in hunting camps in the forests or to hunt buffalo on the prairie. There they built smaller, portable dome homes, known as **wigwams**. These small, temporary structures could be built in less than a day.

To build a wigwam, men placed young, flexible trees in the ground in an oval shape about fourteen feet by twenty feet. They pulled the trees together in arch while women tied the frame together with ropelike wood fibers. The builders covered the wigwam frame with bark or woven reed mats and covered the doorway with an animal hide. In the center of the wigwam an open fireplace kept the family warm.

Bountiful Lakes

The Great Lakes stretch nearly one thousand miles across North America from east to west. Dozens of Native American tribes lived side by side along the shoreline. Although they spoke different languages and sometimes fought with one another, they shared many ideas and ways of life. And for thousands of years, the Great Lakes and surrounding shores provided everything the Native Americans needed to live.

Chapter Two

Family Life

The Native Americans of the Great Lakes put a high value on family life. They believed that every tribe member was part of a larger extended family. For this reason, everyone within a tribe helped family, friends, and other members of the community. And everyone had jobs to do.

Grandmothers and grandfathers, called **elders**, watched the children and acted as teachers. Boys and girls learned by listening to their elders tell stories around the fire. Children learned to take care of themselves by helping their parents perform chores around the home. If some-one fell sick, everyone in the community donated food, clothing, and shelter.

In Great Lakes societies, women were farmers and men were hunters and fishermen. Men and women helped one another perform their jobs, however. The men cleared farmland by cutting down trees and burning away the stumps. When this was done, women planted, weeded, and harvested the crops. They also cooked and preserved the food and sometimes hunted and fished.

Boys and Girls

In Native American society, boys learned to perform the tasks of their fathers. Men taught boys to shape stones

Iroquois men and women plant crops and prepare food. Cooperation within the community was an important part of Iroquois culture.

into arrowheads, axes, and knives for hunting. Boys learned the art of making bows and arrows and how to shoot them straight. Young boys played war games with pretend war clubs made from cornstalks and practiced hunting with tiny bows and arrows.

By the time a boy was ten or twelve, he would spend days alone in the woods hunting. When a boy killed his first large animal, the family celebrated with a feast.

Girls worked with their mothers, learning the tasks needed for farming and cooking. They were also taught to make clothes, cooking vessels, and other household items. Older girls cared for younger children, the sick, and their elders.

Winter and Spring

For all the people of the lakes, daily life revolved around the seasons. In the winter, men hunted deer and other animals. When the snow was deep, they wore snowshoes to move along the paths through the woods and beside the lakes.

Although the lakes were often frozen in winter, men chopped fishing holes in the thick ice with axes. Fishermen either caught fish with spears or trapped them

An Iroquois hunter prepares to spear a moose. The Iroquois were skilled hunters.

in nets dropped through the ice holes. Some used special herbs and carved lures to attract large numbers of fish.

In spring, entire villages moved to the woods to gather syrup from maple trees. Each family had its own stand of maple trees, which they called sugar bush. To tap the trees, a gash was made a few feet off the ground in each tree trunk. A spout made from cedar wood was hammered into the cut, and the sap would trickle into a birch-bark pail beneath the spout. After each tree was drained, the sap was collected and poured into an even larger birch-bark container.

Rocks heated over a campfire were dropped into the filled container, bringing the sap to a boil. The heat

A Native American woman boils pots of maple sap to make syrup.

reduced the liquid, first to syrup then to sugar. When each family had a year's supply of maple sugar, the tribe broke camp and returned to their village.

After the maple harvest, people held ceremonies with prayers and feasts. Fish were roasted on fires or boiled in cornmeal stew. Some were dried and mixed with maple sugar or cranberries. This sweetened fish was packed away into birch-bark containers for later use.

Planting Crops

At the end of the maple sugar and fishing seasons, the final frosts of May gave way to summer farming season. At that time, tribes returned to their villages to plant crops.

Each family had its own garden. Men would till the soil with axes, bones, or any tool that would break the ground. Some made wooden hoes, others used the shoulder blades from a large deer or moose. Once the soil was turned over, women planted seeds for corn, beans, and squash in rows of small clusters called hillocks. After the seeds were sown, a spiritual leader, or shaman, would appeal to the spirits for a bountiful harvest.

Much of the food grown in gardens was preserved for use later in the year. Squash was sliced into pieces and smoked or dried in the sun. Corn was dried and stored whole or ground into meal. Extra corn was stored in underground storage areas lined with birch bark.

Making Beautiful Items

When not preparing food, women and young girls wove many kinds of beautiful baskets. These were used to carry, serve, and store food. Sieve baskets were used to sift finely ground cornmeal. Women also carved spoons, bowls, pitchers, and other kitchen utensils out of wood. They decorated the utensils with carvings of animals such as

Iroquois Crafts

- A wampum belt, made of shells and beads, was given as a symbol of peace and understanding between Great Lakes tribes.

- A beaded velvet vest shows the artistic ability of the Iroquois, and was used during religious celebrations and for trade.

- A False Face mask, carved from the bark of a living basswood tree, was used in Iroquois ceremonies to heal sickness and to bring good luck.

- Stone sculptures represent the importance of nature and spirituality in Iroquois culture, and were often given as offerings to spirits.

hawks or beavers. Special items had carved images of people hugging each other.

Women and girls also made clothing and moccasins out of plant fiber and animal skins. They decorated the clothing with natural materials such as porcupine quills and moose hair. They braided or embroidered the decorations in artistic designs of great beauty.

Building Canoes

While women made baskets and clothing, men built canoes. Canoes were very important because Great Lakes tribes did not have horses or carriages. Canoes allowed people to travel along lakes and rivers for trading, fishing, hunting ducks and geese, and gathering wild rice. Canoes could be from twelve to forty feet long. Shorter canoes could carry two adults, while the longest ones could move up to thirty people.

The tribes of the Great Lakes relied on the canoe because they did not have horses.

To make large, heavy canoes, called dugouts, men pounded stakes into a large tree until it split in half. The wood inside the log was burned and dug out with axes and other scrapers. After many days of hard work, a large passenger area was carved into the log.

Lighter canoes, both large and small, were made with white birch bark. To make a birch-bark canoe, men used hammers and wedges to shape cedar saplings into a canoe frame. Women stripped the bark off birch trees and sewed it onto the framework with thread made from spruce roots. Spruce or pine sap was used to seal the canoe and make it waterproof.

Life for Children

Children also learned to make things. Little girls made dolls out of wood, corn husks, and leather and sewed clothes for them. Boys made little bows and arrows. Boys and girls made spinning tops, feather darts, and other toys. They used sticks for bats and made balls out of stone, wood, stuffed animal skin, pinecones, and large seeds.

In summer, the children played games such as follow the leader or leapfrog. In winter, they listened to stories around the fire. Whatever the season, there was always plenty to do and much to learn while growing up in a Native American tribe around the Great Lakes.

Chapter Three

Beliefs and Ceremonies

The people of the Great Lakes were deeply religious. They believed that nature was full of spirits. These spirits could help people or harm them, depending on how they treated the spirits. They believed the spirits lived within every plant, animal, and rock and in wind, clouds, thunder, and more. The people prayed to these spirits and made offerings to them.

Three Sisters

The people of the lakes believed that one Great Spirit gave the tribes three special plants: corn, beans, and squash. Three spirits supported these crops and helped them to grow. The three spirits were called the "Three Sisters": the Spirit of Corn, the Spirit of Beans, and the Spirit of Squash.

Every spring the Great Lakes Indians planted corn, beans, and squash next to each other. They saw the plants as three beautiful women who loved each other and were very happy to live together. The corn supported the tendrils of the beans, and the beans returned health-giving nutrients to the soil. The squash kept most insects away, but its bright yellow flowers attracted

Legendary Iroquois hero Hiawatha battles fire-breathing serpents. The Great Lakes Indians believed that nature was full of spirits.

helpful bees to pollinate the flowers. The leaves of the plants were the sisters' clothing, which rustled in the wind during the growing season.

Sacred Names

The people of the lakes believed that their spiritual journey began at birth and lasted their entire lives. When a baby was born, the parents asked a respected elder to give the child a sacred name. This name would bring the blessings of the spirits. Often the name came to the elder in a dream. The naming ceremony was held when the child was a month old. Family and friends came to watch as the elder counted all the blessings that he or she had enjoyed in life. By giving the child a name, the elder was also giving the child this good fortune. After giving the name and praying for the child to have long life and good health, everyone enjoyed a feast.

The ceremonial name was very spiritual and was almost never used in daily life. Instead the child was called by a nickname. For example, a very spry little girl might be called Grasshopper. Or a thin boy might be called Little Twig.

The Spirit World

Parents viewed their children as gifts. They treated their children with tenderness and respect. They did not believe in criticizing or hitting children. If children behaved badly, their parents or grandparents told them stories about spirits that might hurt them. For example,

Chief Pontiac addresses Ottawa tribe members during a naming ceremony.

they might be told that the spirit of the owl would carry them off if they refused to quiet down and go to sleep at night. Or if they went into a dangerous part of the forest, an elder wearing a mask of a scary spirit might chase them away.

Grandparents also taught children about the spirits, the creation of the world, and tribal history through songs and stories. Children used the subjects of these stories in paintings, carvings, and other artwork.

When young people became teenagers, their goal was to have a vision or special dream that would give the rest of their lives special meaning. This search was called a vision quest. When teens went on vision quests, they stayed alone in the woods without food until a dream or vision came to them. These were often delivered by special **guardian** spirits called manitous, who watch over people, animals, and plants.

A vision quest was one of the deepest religious experiences in a person's life. This vision, however, was rarely spoken of. A child might discuss it with his or her father or the tribe's spiritual leader.

False Face Society

The faces of spirits were often carved into special masks. These were used in many ceremonies by the people of the lakes. Some Iroquois tribes used scary masks called "False Faces" in magic rituals to cure sickness and bad luck.

Iroquois tribes used False Face masks during magic healing rituals.

A masked Cayuga elder dances during a traditional healing ceremony.

When a ceremony was performed, members of the False Face Society came into a longhouse wearing their magic masks. They circled around the person to be healed, dancing, shaking rattles, and chanting. Others mixed medicine with ashes from the fire pit and blew them on the patient through the mask.

If the sick person got better, he or she could become a member of the False Face Society. To do so, the person carved a mask into the bark of a living basswood tree or hired an artist to help. The mask was then cut away from the tree, hollowed out from behind, and painted. Each mask was different from every other one. Some had locks of animal hair, scowling eyes, and tongues that stuck out and waggled around. Others had huge, pointy

Great Lakes Indians dance around a fellow tribe member during a medicine ceremony.

noses; crooked mouths with huge lips; or sharp, panther-like teeth.

People healed by the False Faces often asked them to renew the healing by repeating the dances during tribal ceremonies. The False Faces also explained the meaning of dreams and held rituals and ceremonies throughout the year.

Medicine and Dreams

The Algonquian tribes also had societies for healing. These groups were formed by those who had similar dreams or visions. For example, several people who had dreams about bears might form a special healing society. Dreams were important because the people of the lakes believed that these visions could keep them healthy.

In many medicine ceremonies, people told each other their dreams and stories to promote good behavior as a key to good health. Their dreams, visions, and stories brought the power of the spirits to life. Ceremonies to make good medicine also included feasts, singing, dancing in masks and costumes, and the music of drums, rattles, and whistles. Men, women, and children took part in these festivities.

The Ojibwa created a special item called a dream catcher to help separate good dreams from bad dreams. Dream catchers were made by bending a twig into a circle and weaving a spiderweb pattern in the middle. A hole in the middle of the web allowed good dreams to pass through to the dreamer. Bad dreams got tangled up in the web and were burned up by the sun at the first light of day.

Dances
Medicine ceremonies included many kinds of dances, such as dream dances, war dances, and peace dances. The Jingle Dress Dance was for healing, while the Bear Dance and Buffalo Dance celebrated successful hunts.

Iroquois men, women, and children join hands during a dance celebration.

To celebrate successful harvests, there were dances dedicated to plants such as the Corn Dance.

In winter and in war or hunting ceremonies, men were the performers. In summer and in harvest ceremonies, women were the performers. Dancers circled around in large groups, with a running step or stomp. This was done in time to responsive singing, when two groups respond to each other in song, or a group responds to a song leader. These group celebrations brought many people together, often from different tribes. They helped the people of the lakes to live together in peace and harmony.

A Trail Through the Sky

The people of the lakes danced, sang, and celebrated the spirits in hundreds of ways. And belief in the spirits continued beyond death. When a person died, his or her soul was said to follow the spirits on a trail through the sky, past the stars of the Milky Way to heaven. In this way people lived forever with the spirits that had watched over them from the time they were born.

Chapter Four

Conflict with Settlers

Native Americans lived along the Great Lakes for more than ten thousand years before the arrival of outsiders. In the early 1700s, boats and canoes began to sail into the Great Lakes carrying men from Europe.

The first known explorers came in 1608, when Samuel de Champlain and a small party of men sailed into the Great Lakes looking for beaver skins. Though there were hundreds of thousands of native people living in the area, Champlain claimed the lands for France and gave the rivers and lakes French names.

Trade Goods

At first, contact between Native Americans and Europeans benefited both. The people of the lakes were eager to trade with the French so they could obtain European **muskets**. In addition to firearms, European traders offered fishhooks, brass kettles, metal knives, axes, sewing needles, and other goods that made daily life easier for the Native Americans.

The people of the lakes showed the Europeans how to grow corn, pumpkins, beans, and squash. They also taught them where to find wild nuts and berries and how to hunt animals in the forests.

French explorer Samuel de Champlain attacks a tribe of Great Lakes Indians. Champlain claimed much of the land surrounding the lakes for France.

Disease and War

Unknowingly, the Europeans also brought deadly diseases into Native American villages. Native Americans had little **resistance** to diseases such as smallpox, measles, and cholera. Outbreaks of these diseases ravaged native populations.

In addition to spreading disease, the Europeans changed the relationships between the tribes. Some weaker tribes were given muskets in trade for furs, while stronger tribes were ignored. For example, the Huron were given guns by the French. They used these to kill their enemies, the once-powerful Mohawk, who did not have firearms.

The Iroquois were supplied with guns by the English. In 1648 the Iroquois Nation attacked the Huron. They killed the people as they ran into the forest and raided the villages and burned them down. By the end of 1649, the few survivors of the Huron nation were starving and dying of disease. The Six Nations of the Iroquois League took over the Great Lakes fur trade that had once belonged to the Huron.

In the 1600s and 1700s England and France fought a series of wars for control of the Great Lakes. The Iroquois usually fought for the English, while the Algonquian tribes sided with the French. By the time the British finally defeated the French in 1760, many nations of Native American people were almost completely wiped out.

Champlain, backed by an army of Huron, fires on an Iroquois village.

The American Revolution

By the 1770s America's East Coast was lined with cities, villages, and towns. Large cities such as New York and Boston were centers of trade with Europe. Goods included animal skins, fish, timber, minerals, and farm products taken from land that once belonged to the people of the lakes. As the number of Europeans grew, tribes in the region were evicted from their homelands. They were forced to move into the western Great Lakes region where they clashed with tribes who already lived there.

George Washington (right) signs a treaty. After the Revolutionary War ended, many Iroquois chiefs were tricked into signing treaties that opened Iroquois land to American settlers.

In 1775 American colonists on the East Coast began a revolution against their British rulers. Four of the six tribes of the Iroquois League sided with the British in the Revolutionary War and helped them destroy American settlements in western New York and Pennsylvania. George Washington, commander in chief of the American army, sent soldiers to raid and burn down forty Iroquois villages and most of their crops. The Iroquois lost their power, and the people starved.

When a peace treaty was signed in 1783, Great Britain surrendered the homelands of Great Lakes tribes to the new government of the United States of America.

Broken Treaties

To the new settlers in the United States, the area around the Great Lakes was known as the Northwest Territory. The U.S. Army and its government representatives called Indian agents poured into the Northwest Territory. Chiefs were given large amounts of alcohol and food and tricked into signing treaties that opened the land to American settlers. These chiefs could not read or write, much less understand the complicated legal language of the treaties. And the chiefs almost never had permission to make decisions on behalf of the other members of their tribe.

As the years passed, the American government took control of more and more land and put it up for sale. American settlers moved into the longhouses and planted crops in Native American cornfields. When some of the Native Americans refused to leave their homelands, military force was used to enforce the treaties.

By the 1850s, the Great Lakes tribes were split up and confined to tiny areas of land called **reservations**. Some reservations were built on ancient tribal homelands.

Chippewa children pose for a photograph. By the 1850s, the Great Lakes tribes had been split up and sent to live on reservations.

More than 110,000 Native Americans live on reservations in the Great Lakes region.

Others were created in Oklahoma, Kansas, Iowa, and elsewhere. In these places traditional methods of farming and hunting were impossible. This led to conditions of extreme poverty and starvation for the people of the lakes.

People of the Lakes Today

Today, more than 110,000 Native Americans live on reservations in the Great Lakes regions of New York, Michigan, Wisconsin, and Minnesota. Another 170,000 Indians live in the Great Lakes regions of Canada.

Native Americans on some reservations face many problems, such as unemployment. In the past twenty years, however, several tribes have opened casinos on reservations. In some states, such as Michigan and Minnesota, these gaming operations have brought great

A Mohawk man and boy wear traditional clothing during an Iroquois celebration.

wealth to the tribes for the first time in nearly four hundred years. With money from casinos, tribes have built homes, hospitals, roads, and other improvements. They have also revived their ancient traditions in dances, music, art, and stories. And many people continue to hunt, fish, and gather from the land, rivers, and lakes of their ancestors.

Respect for Nature

Fishing is still a great source of income for some tribes, especially those who make their home in the western

Many Great Lakes Indians, such as this Chippewa fisherman, still practice the traditions of their ancestors.

part of the Great Lakes. Some tribes have worked to protect and restore their environment. For example, the Keweenaw Bay Indian Community in northern Michigan works with the U.S. Fish and Wildlife Service to restore trout in the Great Lakes.

The people of the lakes have always respected nature and shown thanks for the plants and animals that provide food, shelter, clothing, and medicine. Although they now live in the modern world, these ancient values are still alive today among the people of the lakes.

Glossary

council: A group of people who come together to talk and make decisions.

elder: A well-respected older member of a family, tribe, or community.

guardian: One who guards, watches over, or protects.

musket: A heavy, large gun used from the late-sixteenth through the eighteenth century.

reservation: A tract of land set apart by the federal government for use by Native American people.

resistance: The ability of a person's body to defend itself against disease.

wigwam: A Native American dwelling built with an arched framework overlaid with bark, hides, or mats.

For Further Exploration

Michael Johnson, *American Woodland Indians.* London, England: Reed International Books, 1994. This book gives a short history of each main Algonquian and Iroquois tribe. It includes photos of houses, clothing, and art and illustrations of different styles of dress.

Bobbie Kalman, *Nations of the Western Great Lakes.* New York: Crabtree, 2003. An introduction to the traditions in the daily lives of the natives of the western Great Lakes and how contact with European immigrants changed their lives.

Lisa Sita, *Indians of the Northeast: Traditions, History, Legends, and Life.* Philadelphia: Courage Books, 1997. This book describes the daily lives, ceremonies, stories, and history of the native people who lived along the East Coast of the United States and around the Great Lakes.

Carl Waldman, *Encyclopedia of Native American Tribes.* New York: Facts On File, 1988. Descriptions of the Northeast culture area, the Algonquian, Iroquoian, and Siouan language families and the history, lifeways, art, and religions of individual Native American tribes.

Niki Walker, *Life in an Anishinabe Camp.* New York: Crabtree, 2003. An introduction to the culture, customs, and daily life of the largest tribe in the Great Lakes area, the Anishinabe.

Index

alcohol, 35
Algonquian language, 6, 11
American Revolution, 35
Anishinabe, 11

baskets, 19
beans, 23-24
Bear Dance, 29
birch bark, 22
boys, 15-16
buffalo, 12, 13
Buffalo Dance, 29

canoes, 21-22
casinos, 37, 39
Cayuga, 8
ceremonies
  by False Face Society, 27, 28
  for farming, 30
  for hunting, 29
  medicine, 28-29
  naming, 24-25
Champlain, Samuel de, 31
chiefs, 9-10, 35
children
  education of, 15-17
  role of, 15
  toys and games of, 22
  treatment of, 25-26
  work done by, 19, 21
Chippewa. *See* Ojibwa
clothing, 21
copper, 12
corn, 19, 23-24

Corn Dance, 30
crafts, 19, 21

Dakota language, 12
dances, 29-30
death, 30
diseases, 32
dreamcatchers, 29
dreams, 28, 29
dugouts, 22

elders, 15, 24-25
England, 32, 33
environment, protection of, 40
European diseases, 32
explorers, 31

False Face Society, 26-28
families, 15
farming
  ceremonies for, 30
  by Fox and Sac, 13
  jobs of men and women, 15
  preservation of food grown, 19
  on reservations, 37
  Three Sisters and, 19, 23-24
firearms, 31, 32
fishing
  as current source of income, 39-40
  preservation of catch, 19
  in winter, 17-18
Fox, 12-13

France, 31, 32, 33
fur trade, 33, 34

games, 22
girls
  clothing made by, 21
  crafts made by, 19, 21
  education of, 16-17
  government, 9-10
  grain, 11
  Grand Council, 9-10
  grandparents, 15, 26
  Great Lakes, 6
    see also specific lakes
  guns, 31, 32

healing societies, 28-29
homes, 8-9, 13-14
hunting
  animals, 6, 12, 13
  ceremonies for, 29
  on reservations, 37
Huron, 8, 32-33

ice fishing, 17-18
illness
  community response to, 15
  European diseases, 32
  False Face Society and,
    26-28
  healing societies and, 28-29
  role of older girls and, 17
Indian agents, 35
Iroquois League
  government of, 9-10
  homes of, 8-9
  importance of, 6
  Revolutionary War and, 35
  villages of, 8
  war with Huron and, 32-33

Jingle Dress Dance, 29

Lake Erie, 6
Lake Huron, 6
Lake Michigan, 6, 11, 12, 13
Lake Ontario, 6
Lake Superior, 6, 11
Lakota language, 12
languages, 6, 11, 12
longhouses, 8-9, 13

maple syrup, 18-19
medicine ceremonies, 28-29
men
  canoe building and, 21-22
  farming and, 15, 19
  jobs of, 15
  wigwam building and,
    13-14
Menominee, 11-12
Mesquakie. *See* Fox
Michigan, 37, 39
Minnesota, 37, 39
moccasins, 21
Mohawk, 8, 32
muskets, 31, 32

naming ceremonies, 24-25
nature, respect for, 40
Northwest Territory, 35

Ojibwa, 11, 29
Ojibway. *See* Ojibwa
Oneida, 8
Onondaga, 8
Ottawa, 11

People of the Longhouse. *See*
  Iroquois League
Potawatomi, 11
prophecies, 11

Red Earth People. *See* Fox

religion
  beliefs, 23, 30
  ceremonies, 24-25, 27-30
  Three Sisters in, 23-24
  vision quests, 26
reservations, 35, 37, 39-40
Revolutionary War, 35

sachems, 9-10
Sac, 12, 13
Sauk. *See* Sac
seasons
  importance of, 17
  spring activities, 18-19
  summer activities, 13, 22, 30
  winter activities, 13, 17-18
Seneca, 8
settlers, 34
shamans, 19
sickness
  community response to, 15
  European diseases, 32
  False Face Society and,
    26-28
  healing societies and, 28-29
  role of older girls and, 17
Six Nations. *See* Iroquois
  League
snowshoes, 17
spring activities, 18-19
squash, 19, 23-24
sugarbush, 18

summer activities, 13, 22, 30

teenagers, 26
Three Fires tribes, 11
Three Sisters, 19, 23-24
toys, 22
trade, 31, 33, 34
treaties, 35
Tuscarora, 8

unemployment, 37

villages of Iroquois, 8
vision quests, 26

war
  American Revolution, 35
  between tribes, 32-33
Washington, George, 35
wigwams, 13-14
wild rice, 11
Winnebago, 12
winter activities, 13, 17-18
women
  canoe building and, 22
  ceremonies and, 30
  clothing made by, 21
  crafts made by, 19, 21
  farming and, 15, 19
  jobs of, 15

Yellow Earth People. *See* Sac

Picture Credits

Cover: © Hulton Archive
© AAMP, 20 (bottom left, right)
© James L.Amos/CORBIS, 39
© Blackbirch Press, 20 (middle left, right) 34
© Denver Public Library, 21, 36
Chris Jouan, 20
Library of Congress, 13
© David Muench/CORBIS, 7
© Nativestock.com, 9, 16, 17, 18, 24, 26, 27, 29, 37
NOAA, 7 (inset)
© North Wind Picture Archives, 8, 10, 12, 25, 28, 32, 33
© Ted Spiegel/CORBIS, 38

About the Authors

P.M. Boekhoff is an author of more than twenty-five non-fiction books for children. She has written about history, science, and the lives of creative people. In addition, P.M. Boekhoff is an artist who has created murals and theatrical scenic paintings and has illustrated many book covers. In her spare time she paints, draws, writes poetry, and studies herbal medicine.

Stuart A. Kallen is the author of more than 160 nonfiction books for children and young adults. He has written on topics ranging from the theory of relativity to the history of rock and roll. In addition, Mr. Kallen has written award-winning children's videos and television scripts. In his spare time, Stuart A. Kallen is a singer/songwriter/guitarist in San Diego, California.